T0078419

UNIQUELY PECULIAR,
AT THE WELL

UNIQUELY PECULIAR

authorHOUSE®

AuthorHouse™
1663 Liberty Drive
Bloomington, IN 47403
www.authorhouse.com
Phone: 833-262-8899

Published by AuthorHouse 12/10/2020

ISBN: 978-1-6655-0665-6 (sc)
ISBN: 978-1-6655-0666-3 (e)

Library of Congress Control Number: 2020921667

Print information available on the last page.

This book is printed on acid-free paper.

Scripture taken from the King James Version of the Bible.

ACKNOWLEDGEMENT

- ❖ I thank and praise God for giving me His grace and mercy through it all.
- ❖ A special thanks to my children, Preston Harden & Phillip Loken.
- ❖ To all my relatives, friends, Malaby's Crossroads Missionary Baptist Church (Knightdale, NC) and others who have assisted me along this journey sharing their support, either financially, morally, physically and spiritually, I say thank you.
- ❖ I am also grateful to my publishers at AuthorHouse for their patience and guidance.

CONTENTS

INTRODUCTION

Uniquely Peculiar, At the Well is loosely based on the story of the Samaritan woman at the well.

Most people find faith, hope and love thru reading the scriptures and gaining insight pertaining to their own lives. *Uniquely peculiar, At the Well* illustrates this point. In John 4:3-26, KJV, it tells the story of the Samaritan woman going about her chores for the day and along came Jesus at the well. The meeting with Jesus changed her whole life.

As a woman, I can relate to her on a personal level. This book of poetry captures some insight to her feelings, anxieties, worries, and frustrations from my point of view.

As you read these poems, hopefully you will see yourself as a uniquely peculiar person of God.

AT THE WELL

THE SCRIPTURE: JOHN 4:1-26 (KJV)
THE WOMAN AT THE WELL

¹When therefore the Lord knew how the Pharisees had heard that Jesus made and baptized more disciples than John,

²(Though Jesus himself baptized not, but his disciples,)

³He left Judaea, and departed again into Galilee.

⁴And he must needs go through Samaria.

⁵Then cometh he to a city of Samaria, which is called Sychar, near to the parcel of ground that Jacob gave to his son Joseph.

⁶Now Jacob's well was there. Jesus therefore, being wearied with his journey, sat thus on the well: and it was about the sixth hour.

⁷There cometh a woman of Samaria to draw water: Jesus saith unto her, Give me to drink.

⁸(For his disciples were gone away unto the city to buy meat.)

⁹Then saith the woman of Samaria unto him, How is it that thou, being a Jew, askest drink of me, which am a woman of Samaria? for the Jews have no dealings with the Samaritans.

¹⁰Jesus answered and said unto her, If thou knewest the gift of God, and who it is that saith to thee, Give me to drink; thou wouldest have asked of him, and he would have given thee living water.

¹¹The woman saith unto him, Sir, thou hast nothing to draw with, and the well is deep: from whence then hast thou that living water?

¹²Art thou greater than our father Jacob, which gave us the well, and drank thereof himself, and his children, and his cattle?

¹³Jesus answered and said unto her, Whosoever drinketh of this water shall thirst again:

¹⁴ But whosoever drinketh of the water that I shall give him shall never thirst; but the water that I shall give him shall be in him a well of water springing up into everlasting life.

¹⁵ The woman saith unto him, Sir, give me this water, that I thirst not, neither come hither to draw.

¹⁶ Jesus saith unto her, Go, call thy husband, and come hither.

¹⁷ The woman answered and said, I have no husband. Jesus said unto her, Thou hast well said, I have no husband:

¹⁸ For thou hast had five husbands; and he whom thou now hast is not thy husband: in that saidst thou truly.

¹⁹ The woman saith unto him, Sir, I perceive that thou art a prophet.

²⁰ Our fathers worshipped in this mountain; and ye say, that in Jerusalem is the place where men ought to worship.

²¹ Jesus saith unto her, Woman, believe me, the hour cometh, when ye shall neither in this mountain, nor yet at Jerusalem, worship the Father.

²² Ye worship ye know not what: we know what we worship: for salvation is of the Jews.

²³ But the hour cometh, and now is, when the true worshippers shall worship the Father in spirit and in truth: for the Father seeketh such to worship him.

²⁴ God is a Spirit: and they that worship him must worship him in spirit and in truth.

²⁵ The woman saith unto him, I know that Messias cometh, which is called Christ: when he is come, he will tell us all things.

²⁶ Jesus saith unto her, I that speak unto thee am he.

THE WOMAN AT THE WELL

The well wasn't too far.
It was a bit down the road.
She was trying to quench her thirst,
trying to change her mode.

A man was there.
A man not of her kind.
To be seen with Him
was not a good sign.

This man came
to comfort and save the lost.
He came to give her living waters,
no matter what the cost.

He told her about the living waters,
which He so freely gives
to anyone who drinks it,
and who truly wants to live.

She wanted to know
about the living waters of salvation.
Then, He told her about her husbands plus one.
Would this end their conversation?

She tried to contain herself
with His words of revelations.
How could He know all of this?
Who told Him about her personal relations?

He didn't demean or
use words of condemnation.
He said go and sin no more.
She left to begin her transformation.

ODE TO THE WELL

The water in thee, oh well!
I wish the water well!
Wet is the water, oh well!
Wail, wail, the water in the Well!

HE WAS THERE ALL THE TIME

He was there all the time.
Waiting on me.
Did I not see Him?
Was He hiding from me?
Did I seek Him out?
Did I call out His name?
Did I pass by Him?
Did I ignore Him?
He was there all the time.

INSECURE

Am I pretty enough?
What's wrong with me?
Why are you staring at me?
Do I look like funny?

I go along so
I won't be lonely.
I laugh with you so
you won't laugh at me.

I'm not as smart
as I think you are.
I act like I'm having fun.
I'm just playing the part.

I don't say much.
Nobody listens or cares.
I just exist to be,
a body, a hollow shell.

CHANGE

I didn't think I could do it,
not by myself anyway.
I keep stopping and restarting.
Why do I always stray?

I 'm getting better now.
My life has been changed anew.
Thru my prayers and my faith,
I found that I can go through.

My life is changed completely.
New directions are in my path.
Now I know of a true love,
a love that will always last.

The change isn't overnight.
It is really a process.
Everyday I'm learning and leaning,
as I make my faith to faith progress.

THIS TIME WOULD BE DIFFERENT

This time would be different, I've said it many times.
"It won't happen again", was my favorite chime.

This time would be different; I knew it was true love.
He was heaven sent, straight from above.

He seemed to be sincere, I knew him for a while.
He would make a good daddy for my unborn child.

He said he would go to church with me,
something always came up, you see.

At first, He seemed to care.
Now, we're married, he's just there.

He tried to find a job while searching the internet.
He didn't have to leave the house, haven't found one yet.

Yes, he loves me. He tells me all the time.
I believe he wasn't lying. However, I could see signs.

I was working all the time, trying to pay our bills.
His attitude was changing, it was going downhill.

I didn't want to be alone, without a man beside me.
I was trying to make it work, I just wanted a family.

His heart was cold, and his words were harsh.
Heaven sent turned into being a total farce.

This time is different, this has to stop with me.
I have to get away, I have to flee.

This time is different.

LET ME GET SOME WATER

How can I talk to you?
I don't even know what to say.
Just let me get my water
and I'll be on my way.

You don't know what I'm going through.
It's hard to explain, hard to tell.
I just want to get some water
out of the well.

How can you talk to me?
You know the gossip around town.
Let me get my water
I won't make a sound.

Who told you about my life?
I tried to keep it hidden,
with all the gossiping and rumors,
I knew some things were forbidden.

Let me get some water.
Living waters from the Savior,
to quench my thirsty soul,
to change my heart and behavior.

TRYING TO LOVE ME

You let me down so many times.
I wanted to forgive.
My mind couldn't forget
the things I tried to relive.

You set me up for failure,
a fate worse than death.
You knew I couldn't win.
I couldn't help myself.

I tried to get away from you,
thru sex, drugs, and alcohol.
But somehow, I needed you,
you knew, I would call.

My physical features were homely.
Cosmetic enhancements were for a price.
You thought they would make me desirable.
But what did I sacrifice?

You didn't like the clothes I wore
or how I fixed my hair.
You kept trying to please me.
It seemed I didn't' care.

I wanted to tell you that I love you,
so much it hurts my voice.
You know what you must do,
now that you have a choice.

The mirror shows us the outer person,
images that can come and go.
Jesus sees us through His eyes,
Oh, He loves us so.

Now you know the path before you.
Stop looking in the past.
Look forward to Jesus as your Savior,
and not thru some painted glass.

THE WELL

The living waters at the well.
Did I forget to bring my pail?
To overflowed it to the brink,
to quench my thirst, I need a drink.

I NEED A DRINK

It's been a rough week.
So busy, don't even have time to blink.
Everything and everybody are going crazy,
I think I need a drink.

Children not listening.
Hubby and I are on the brink.
The romance is almost gone.
I think I need a drink.

The job is trying at times.
I'm a pion in the ranks.
They are talking about downsizing and layoffs.
I think I need a drink.

The drive home is no better.
People driving with no restraints.
Now, the car in front of me stalls.
I think I need a drink.

I get home in one piece
into the chair, I sink.
I prayed and I read my bible.
Aw, yes, I needed this drink.

A drink to ease my worries.
A drink to erase my complaints.
A drink to calm my fears.
Yes, I needed a drink.

Jesus is the fountain.
The drink to quench my thirst.
The Living Waters of heaven
to break Satan earthly curse.

The well of salvation,
flowing over at the brink.
Fill my cup, Lord,
because, Yes, I need a drink.

THE FIVE.......... OFF TO THE WELL

Yes, I had five.
It didn't start out that way.
You don't know my story.
I have something to say.

I could tell you excuses.
You have heard them all before.
I always wanted to be married.
That's all you need to know.

Getting married was easy.
Love was great at first.
Then our true characters came out.
Things began to get worse.

When each one left, I felt
I could not give up and quit.
My man is still out there.
I'm going to find him, I must admit.

Now, I've divorced a handful.
I have a boyfriend now.
I can't get married again?
No way, No how.

I've got to make it right
A man told me today.
I have been forgiven.
Now, I know the way.

MAKING IT TO THE WELL

I've got to get to the well.
There is someone waiting for me,
to give me the living waters
so that I can be set free.

The road to the well
is winding and long.
But I will be restored
and with Him, I'll belong.

UNREQUITED LOVE, …. BE MY VALENTINE

I created you after my own image, Genesis 1:27
I gave my only son for you, John 3:16
I went to hell and back for you, Acts 2:31
I will never break my promises with you, Philippians 1:6
I will never leave you nor forsake you, Hebrews 13:5
I am with you always, Matthew 28:20
You can talk to me, Isaiah 1:18
I will fight for you, Exodus 14:14
I will never change on you, Hebrews 13:8
I don't care about outward appearances, Proverbs 31:30
I am your comforter, John 14:18
I will supply your every need, Philippians 4:19
I care for you, 1 Peter 5:7
I know you are not perfect, Romans 3:23
I will never lie to you, Numbers 23:19
You can trust me, Proverbs 3:5
I will give you joy, 1 Peter 1:8
I have a place prepared for you, John 14:2
I have a gift for you, Romans 6:23
I love you, John 3:16
…….JESUS

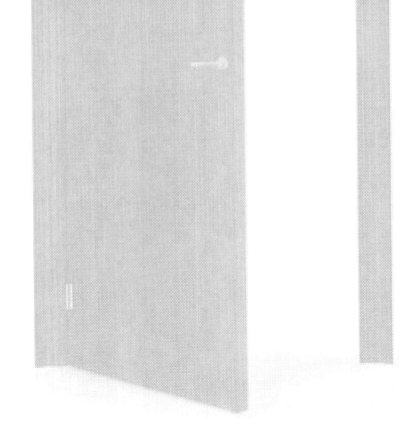

AND OTHER POEMS

THE DOOR

I only had to get to the door.
There were so many things in front of me,
blocking my way.
Anger, pride, and resentment got me there.
The mirror of lies made it look like it was too far for me to make it.
Potholes of Sin was scattered all around.
Unforgiveness, doubt and fear were oil spots, I was going nowhere fast.
The door was blocked by the past, reminding me of the guilt.
I had to lay aside every weight to get to the door

John 10:9 I am the **door**: by me if any man enter in, he shall be saved, and shall go in and out, and find pasture.

Hebrews 12:1 Wherefore seeing we also are compassed about with so great a cloud of witnesses, let us lay aside every weight, and the sin which doth so easily beset us, and let us run with patience the race that is set before us,

HEARING

I lost my hearing.
The words sounds blurred.
I am no sure of what you said
or of what I heard.

Huh, or please repeat
is my chant back to you.
Listening to what you say
is not easy to do.

The sounds of letters,
becoming words and speech.
Hopefully with the hearing aids
I can hear you speak.

Piercing whistling sounds
or the sirens of the ambulance,
hurt my ears to the extreme
I can only hear the silence.

I used to go out and be with friends,
but noise gives way to deaf matters.
I stay inside to stop trying to hear
the confusion brought by hearing chatter.

YOU ARE MY FRIEND

You were there when I needed you,
and even when I didn't.
You were there when I was sick
or sad or bedridden.

You knew my life struggles.
My disappointments and pain.
Yet, you loved me anyway.
You kept me from going insane.

You encourage me with the Word of God.
You prayed for me all the time
You were always with me,
When others were not so kind.

We got upset with each other,
no backing down or giving in.
Not allowing the other to quit,
a true friend among friends.

You are my friend

THE ROCK

It's a rough life for me. Most consider me strong.
I get thrown around hurting people and breaking bones.

They are curious about me at the beach.
They kick me along in the streets.

Sometimes I'm dirty, broken, and cracked.
They throw me in the ocean, but the waves bring me back.

I helped Peter build the church.
I assisted the birds in constructing their perch.

I may feel hard and sometimes cold,
but underneath I'm just a pebble acting bold.

I KICKED A ROCK TODAY...AN INCONSEQUENTIAL DAY

I kicked a rock today.
Wonder where it went?
Did it just keep rolling?
Did it break and scatter?

Why did I kick it?
Did it hurt me in some way?
Was it too big for me to go around?
Did it cause me to trip and splatter?

Did I kick it to ease my pain?
Did I kick it out of anger?
It didn't make me happy.
It just got me madder.

Did I kick it to rattle my brain or
make my thoughts go away?
Did it help to bring up memories
of days when things were better?

Was it really bothering me?
Was it blocking my path?
Was it daring me to kick it,
to break it and shatter?

Did it crush under the pressure?
Did it return to dust?
Did it hit another rock?
Does it really matter?

FAITH

They say you can't see it, But I do every day.
In some shape, form or fashion, I see it in some way.

We sit in a chair, we walk, drive or ride.
We discuss the next day agenda, and as we put this day aside.

We have a to-do list; our itineraries are all planned out.
Without faith in the future, our future would be in doubt.

Faith is the action of doing, and doing is an action of faith,
one without the other is not open to debate

Faith in our beliefs keeps us on track,
pressing toward our mark not giving us any slack.

Faith in a few things can make you ruler over many things.
Faith can save us, Faith can move mountains,

Faith is the substance of things hope for and the evidence of things not
seen.
It is the needs of tomorrow and it is the wants of our dreams.

Faith

OUR PASTOR

Our pastor preaches the Word of God to the poor, sick and to the lost.
Our pastor preaches Jesus and His resurrection, no matter what the cost.

Our pastor preaches to restore, refresh and renew,
to demonstrate God's Love to me and to you.

Our pastor preaches to tell of His grace and mercy and His miraculous birth,
anointed to proclaim the Gospel here on Earth.

Our pastor preaches to make ready the church for when the bridegroom comes,
showing praises to God, thru prayers, and bible studies and songs.

Our pastor preaches to show by example, forgiveness, and love,
a willing vessel for God and Jesus above.

An unashamed workman, rightly dividing the Word of Truth,
teaching to everyone, adults and to the youth.

Humble in Spirit, compassionate for souls,
helping us to make it to Heaven is the ultimate goal.

Keep singing the songs of Zion and preaching The Word of God,
continue in His presence and living the words of God.

THE CAREGIVER

Her time is given to assisting her loved ones
in the everyday living of life.
Her strength is given by God
as she labors as caregiver, mother, and wife.

She washes their body just as
Mary washed Jesus' feet.
A humbled and holy gesture,
for the saved and the meek.

She wakes up early
with a prayer on her heart.
Giving it all to God
as she does her part.

Her work is never
out of requirement or duty.
It is an intentional choice
she gives gladly, and freely.

Motivated by Love,
her days are hard.
Her hours are long,
yet patience is her song.

She does it not for
notice, ego or fame.
She does it for His Glory
in Jesus' Name.

THE CHURCH

Communing with brothers and sisters in unity.
Hell's gates cannot prevail against it.
Unbinding the chains of Satan.
Reaching the Lost, The Blind, and The Captives.
Caring for the sick, shut-ins and widows.
Hallelujahs, Amens and praises to our GOD!

JESUS

JUSTIFYING
EVERYONE,
SEEING
US
SAVED!

FAREWELL, MY NEWSPAPER!

Farewell, my newspaper,
my morning friend.
Rattling thru your pages
which knew no end.

Extra, Extra, read all about it,
the quieting of that fateful cry.
Black and White And Read all over.
The riddle that would never die.

A long-ago
worldwide trusted source,
gave way to social media,
for you, it had no remorse.

Farewell, my newspaper.
No longer at my doorsteps.
News on my computer, tablet, and cell
is where you will always be kept.

Farewell, my newspaper!

SENIORS ON THE MOVE

We are Seniors on the move,
praying as He lights our way.
Studying to show ourselves approved,
following God's guidance every day.

We are on the move by example.
Jesus is our model.
We're pressing toward the mark,
carrying the gospel.

Encouraging the depressed, and lonely.
We are prayer warriors 24/7.
Lifting up the downtrodden.
Just trying to make it to heaven.

We are moving to the nursing homes,
the streets, the prisons, and the church.
Teaching others about Jesus, His life,
His resurrection and his miraculous birth.

We are moving to make a difference
to the brokenhearted, and the sick.
To comfort the widows and the poor
with a desire for God that won't quit.

Our wisdom comes with age.
Our faith in God keeps us safe and sound.
We're tearing down Satan's strongholds,
because we are on our way, we're heaven-bound.

We are Seniors on the move .

SINGING THE PRAISES OF GOD

Singing the praises of God is what we do.
Singing of His greatness is our testimony to you.

Just as I am, tempted and tried,
I've been buked, and I've been scorned,
but I know He can break every chain,
now, I am free.

Nobody knows the trouble I see but
I can tell you how I got over.

Pass me not oh gentle savior; I want just a closer walk with thee.

Come by here my Lord; It's me, it's me, it's me, O Lord, standing in need
of prayer.

I am never alone because my God is real, I know
because He walks with me, and He talks with me and tells me I am His own.

I am on the battlefield for my Lord because victory is mine and there is
victory in Jesus.

Satan, we're going to tear your kingdom down. Yes, this means war.

Every time I feel the spirit, I will pray.
Because every day with Jesus is sweeter than the day before.

The Lord will make a way somehow. You brought me through this, and
You brought me that.

I am bound for the promised land on my way home and It is well with my
soul.

Thank you, Lord, I want to Thank you, Lord for just one more day.

THE PANDEMIC

The pandemic started with Adam & Eve.
It didn't take long for it to spread.
It leaves the mind without Godly wisdom.
It leaves the soul dead.

 We take precautions against it.
Church, prayers and read the Bible.
But without a sincere heart,
our motives are for show and shallow.

This pandemic is nothing new,
it leaves the world cold.
but thru His grace and mercy,
God is still in control.

THE COVID-19 CHANGE

Business trips and office boards meeting,
we were so busy once before.
The restaurants, and crowed groceries,
out all day, at the clothing stores.

Smiling at each other,
and seeing each other laugh.
Shaking hands, hugging and kissing,
not knowing that this won't last.

Now we stay locked up in our homes
on conference calls, and video chats.
Trying to keep busy using
soap, sanitizers and masks.

Parents have become teachers.
Grandparents have become isolated.
Children have become bored.
Office buildings have become evacuated.

They say it is the new normal,
but It's only for a season.
God is still running the show.
He has His reasons.

Printed in the United States
By Bookmasters